ISBN 978-1-331-43339-2
PIBN 10189580

This book is a reproduction of an important historical work. Forgotten Books uses
state-of-the-art technology to digitally reconstruct the work, preserving the original format
whilst repairing imperfections present in the aged copy. In rare cases, an imperfection in
the original, such as a blemish or missing page, may be replicated in our edition. We do,
however, repair the vast majority of imperfections successfully; any imperfections that
remain are intentionally left to preserve the state of such historical works.

1 MONTH OF
FREE
READING

at
www.ForgottenBooks.com

By purchasing this book you are eligible for one month membership to ForgottenBooks.com, giving you unlimited access to our entire collection of over 700,000 titles via our web site and mobile apps.

To claim your free month visit:
www.forgottenbooks.com/free189580

Similar Books Are Available from
www.forgottenbooks.com

The
Grey Feet of the Wind

Poems by
CATHAL O' BYRNE

New York
Frederick A. Stokes Company
Publishers

Printed by
The Educational Company of Ireland
at
THE TALBOT PRESS,
89 Talbot St., Dublin

CONTENTS

FOREWORD.

The Grey Feet of the Wind sweep o'er
    the bending grasses,
Down the bright meadows in the breezy
    noon,
Leaving behind them where each light foot
    passes
    The track of their Silver Shoon.

So through the dim-lit aisles of Memory's
    Garden
The Grey Winds go dream laden, crooning
    some old, dear tune,
To where the Seneschal, My Heart, a
    Happy Warden
    Keeps each Remembered Rune.

A few of the poems in this volume are re-
printed from THE LANE OF THE THRUSHES.
The others have appeared in the following
papers and magazines, and through the
courtesy of the Editors and Proprietors are
republished here: "The Messenger" (New
York), "America" (New York), "The Gaelic
American" (New York). "The New York Even-
ing Times," "The Sunday Times" (New York),
"Ave Maria" (Notre Dame, Indiana), "The
New World" (Chicago), "The Southern Cross"
(Buenos Ayres), and "The Westminster
Budget" (London).

For musical rights apply through the
Publishers.

THE GREY FEET OF THE WIND.

I FOLLOWED in the track of the Grey Feet
    of The Wind,
Where Black Clouds ran across the Moon.
    adown a Sullen Sky
Like a Herd of Frightened Cattle with
    Harrying Wolves behind
And dark pines stretched gaunt arms to
    me as I went shuddering by.

Past many a Grey Cairn Stone I went—
    the mad wind whistling on—
With the Dead Dust of Years clogging my
    eyes and breath,
Till White Spears flashed in the East, and
    the Red Wind of Dawn
Fanned into flame the Passion Fires, the
    Fires of Life and Death.

1

(D 338)

On where Night's dream fires are quencht,
    and Dawn's wide gates unclose,
'Through cool white mists of Morning, out
    from the World away,
To where the Sapphire turns to Flame, the
    Ruby burns in the Rose,
And the Silver Bars that are tipped with
    Stars melt in the Heart of Day.

I followed in the track of the Grey Feet
    of The Wind,
'O, Dew-wet Wind of Morning, what word
    have ye to say?
'O, Life is bitter, and Love is sweet, and
    only Death is kind,
For Life is Hope, and Love is Life, and
    Life is Death alway.

THE FAIRY WELL OF SLEMISH.

'TWAS the grey of the evening when Shaun
    came over
  The mountain's shoulder by Torloch's
    Tower,
Like clustered pearls lay the dew on the
    clover,
  One pale star burned thro' that dew-
    grey hour.

He came to the Fairy Well of Slemish,
  In the cool, green moss like a gem it lay;
And he thought of the girl without blame
    or blemish,
  The dark, proud girl who had said him
    " Nay."

He stooped to drink of the sweet well-
      water;
  To the moss grown stones he bent a knee.
" Oh, sweet as the kiss of a High King's
      Daughter,
  Is the Well of Forgetfulness," said he.

" Oh, sweeter far than the sweet well water
  Are the lips of Love," said a voice, and
      he
Looked up and beheld the High King's
      Daughter,
  Of Tir-na-noge in the Realms of Shee.

" Drink three deep draughts," said the
      High King's Daughter,
  "And the wish of your heart I can give,"
      said she,
"Oh I have drunk deep of the sweet well-
      water,
  And the wish of my heart is yourself,"
      said he.

He kissed her lips, as the poppies scarlet,
 He made her heart on his heart to lie,
While a rain of tears that one gold star
  let
 Fall thro' the dusk down the opal sky.

Then away with them over the purple
  heather,
 By dark fir-wood and by starlit brae;
Their silvery laughter ringing together
 And nor sight nor sign of them since
  that day.

THE MAN WHO WENT THE ROADS.

I DANCED on a day in Connacht
  By the cross in a market square,
And the young girls came to the doorways,
  A piper was playing there.
And an old man praised my dancing,
  Said it was just to his mind,
Oh! 'twas good to be dancing in Connacht
  Out in the sun and the wind.

I told a story in Leinster
  To a man at a wayside gate,
Of Da Derga and Emain Macha,
  And Tara's sorrowful fate.
But the man looked out o'er his pastures,
  His face never lost its gloom,
Ochon! but Leinster is lonely
  And cold as an empty room.

6

THE MAN WHO WENT THE ROADS

I made a poem in Munster
    When the dreams in my head ran wild,
'Twas where a turf fire smouldered
    And a woman sang to her child
At the end of an Autumn evening
    After the bit and the sup.
My hand! 'Tis a Munster welcome
    For lifting a lad's heart up.

I sang a song in Ulster
    In the narrow streets of a town,
And the people passed sullen and silent—
    Some looked at me with a frown.
But a *young* man praised my singing,
    Said it was grand and the like,
And put his arm round my shoulder—
    'Twas a song of a *gun* and a *pike*.

A SILENT MOUTH.

O LITTLE green leaf on the bough, you hear
    the lark in the morn,
You hear the grey feet of the wind stir in
    the shimmering corn,
You hear low down in the grass
The singing Shee as they pass;
Do you ever hear, O little green flame!
My loved one calling, calling, whispering
    my name?

O little green leaf on the bough like my
    lips you must ever be dumb,
For a maiden must never speak till Love
    to her heart says " Come!"
A mouth in its silence is sweet,
But my heart cries loud when we meet,
And I turn my head with a bitter sigh,
When the boy who has stolen my love,
    unheeding goes by.

S

I have made my heart as the stones in the
    street for his tread,
I have made my love as the shadow that
    falls from his dear gold head.
But the stones with his footsteps ring,
And the shadow keeps following,
And just as the quiet shadow goes ever
    beside or before
So must I go silent and lonely and loveless
    for ever and evermore.

HOW DIARMUID GOT HIS LOVE-SPOT.

Conan and Osgar and Diarmuid slept
Sweetly and soundly without dream or
　　fret,
Until a great light gleamed in the chamber,
As if a torch to the roof were set.

And they wakened wide-eyed, and wonder-
　　ing, saw,
Like a yellow star through the purple
　　gloom,
In her young youth's beauty, without robe
　　or raiment,
A maiden standing within the room.

And the flame of her loveliness glowed and
　　shone,
And her shadow lay o'er the rush-strewn
　　space,

10

Like a shining candle, where no light was
burning,
Her hair's bright radiance filled the place.

For a while she stood by the bed-post tall,
Nor eye that had seen could ever forget,
Then like a pink shell on a foam-crest
tossing,
She slipped 'neath the light, white coverlet.

Then Conan stood out on the rush-strewn
floor,
And his heart was glad with love's sweet
pain,
" Go back to your bed," said the maiden
gently,
" I belonged to you once, but can never
again."

Then Osgar stood out on the rush-strewn
floor,
" And where are you going?" the maiden
said,

" I've a mind to go where my heart is
    going" :
" I belonged to you once, but that day is
    dead."

Then Diarmuid stood out on the rush-
    strewn floor,
" And where are you going? O, Man of
    Truth !
I may not be yours for the having or taking,
I belonged to you once, my name is Youth.

" But come and kneel by the bed-post here,
And I'll put a love-spot upon your face;
That, seeing once, no woman forever
Shall love withhold for a moment's space."

Then she put her hand 'tween his level
    brows,
And she sighed as she placed the mark
    above,
Maybe she dreamed of his great undoing
By the gift unsought, of a woman's love.

THE MOTHER O' SHAUN.

SHAUN stood six feet or so, with his head
    up near the rafter,
He be to stoop when he came in the door,
Shuttin' out the sunshine, but his cheery
    hearty laughter
Brought more brightness than the streak
    o' light that lay along the floor.
And ye'd think it was a hive o' honey
    bees among the heather.
Or ye'd think it was a ring o' bells
    through sunny summer air,
An' ye'd maybe think 'twas bees an' bells
    amoiderin' together.
But it be to be his heart that made the
    music everywhere.

An' I wish I'd see him standin' in the
    shadow there above me,
And see his white teeth gleam, his blue
    eyes glow,
Though the other boys are near to me to
    cheer me an' to love me.
Shaun had the hearty ways with him
    they'll never, never know.
But the big worl' called him always, its
    wonder called him loudly,
So he bent his head with his loving kiss
    beneath the lintel low.
An' I prayed " God guard him always "
    an' I prayed " God bless him "
    proudly,
I'm his mother, ye'll be mindin', an' I
    knew he be to go.

AWAY FROM IRELAND.

Though I'm far and very far away from
    Ireland,
There's a knot of purple thistles on a cliff
    above the sea,
Like a silver censer flaming between the
    sky and me,
The blood-red bells of fuchsias swing
    around a cabin door,
Where the yellow sunlight showers down
    to flood the earthen floor,
  Far away, and very far away in Ireland.

Though I'm far and very far away from
    Ireland,
There's a grey rock 'mid the heather where
    the bees hum all the day,
Adown its mossy shoulder trails a crimson
    briar spray,

15

Like a craobh of ancient Ogham locked
    beneath Time's magic key,
But the beauty of its message is as clear
    as dawn to me,
  Far away, and very far away in Ireland.

Though I'm far and very far away from
    Ireland,
There's a turf cart standing idle in a quiet
    village street,
The hens roosting on its axle in the shadow
    from the heat,
There's a barefoot boy beside it looking out
    towards the sea.
And the birds have far more trouble for
    the morrow's morn than he,
  Far away, and very far away in Ireland.

Though I'm far and very far away from
    Ireland,
If the black hand of misfortune had
    gripped my heavy heart.

If the red blisters of disgrace had made
    my pale cheek smart,
I'd little heed the trouble or the blame that
    lay on me,
If climbing on a white road between golden
    whins I'd be
Far away, and very far away in Ireland.

GRAINNE.
AFTER THE DEATH OF DIARMUID.

FORTH from the twilight of a wood she
     came,
Where blossoming isles of purple hare-bells
     gleamed,
Set in a shimmering, sunflecked sea of
     green.
Fair was her face as the deep rose of the
     dawn,
And lithe her form as the lake grasses tall,
That whispered of her beauty to the breeze,
Tear-stained her cheeks—rock roses washed
     with spray,
Great haunting memories dwelt of happier
     days
Deep in the shadowy depths of her sad eyes,
Her hair flowed down, a gleaming golden
     wave,

O'er snowy fold and fold of her white robe,
Like sun-kissed water on a silver strand,
Its ripples streaming on a soft west wind,
Were mirrored in the wide, weed-laden
lake
Where she passed by. The silent, sleepy
birds,
Thinking the sun had backward from the
West
Turned in his course, and with his shafts
of gold
Had stabbed the heart of the dim, silent
pool,
Burst into music, and a shower of song,
Fell through the leaves to greet this new
day star.
Twin dew-wet quickenberries were her lips,
one word,
Came through their rosy portals, " Diar-
muid,"
It rang adown the dusky, flower-strewn
glades,

Through aisles of forest trees, of mighty
    oaks,
Of quivering aspen, and of silver larch,
And stately giant pines, and hazel groves;
The melody of murmuring waters caught
    the sound,
And chaunted " Diarmuid " to the mossy
    stones.
Down to the depths of the calm woods it
    sank,
And up through arching green to the broad
    sky,
Through traceries of bronze and blue above,
And far beneath of glimmering gold and
    green,
The Nightingale caught up the new, sweet
    sound,
And for an instant held it in her throat,
Then flung it on the silence of her bower,
Where as it fell it burst in silver rain,
And scattered to the winds its sparks of
    song.

The myriad songsters caught the glittering
    drops,
And flying with the gems throughout the
    wood,
Sang " Diarmuid" in silver syllables, till
    the notes,
Forming one grand, sweet chord, went
    echoing
Through the vast aisles and gold-green
    garden ways,
And all the wood rang sweet with
    " Diarmuid,"
Until the hills in pity sent the name
Back to the forest's fringe whereat she
    stood.
And it at length found its true resting-
    place
Deep in the inmost core of her lone heart.

WHEN SEUMAS MAC-AN-REE PLAYED "THE COULIN."

A SECRET heavy sighing stirred the naked
trees
That leaned to listen there in Cushendall,
Sharp and grief-laden was the wet sea-
breeze
Like slender arrows whistling in their
fall.
And as about the strings the bow was
curled
Love sobbed its woe out in a dirge of pain,
A woe that held the weight of all the world
Of love that had been spilt in golden rain.

And in it was the cry of every Gael
That ever yearned, the sund'ring sea
between,
With outstretched arms to raise the misty
veil
That hung between him and " Dark
Rosaleen"

The singing waters mingled with the
    strain,
    Tumbling afar down steep Lurgaidan's
      side,
And soft as southwinds through the
    ripened grain
    Low through Glenariff's glens a Banshee
      cried.

" 'Tis the last glimpse of Erin" sigh the
    strings,
    The foam-fringed wave turns back to kiss
      the shore,
A swift, unbidden teardrop smarts and
    stings,
    A silence long and deep, the song is o'er.
'Twas Ireland's sad fate was in the
    wailing—
    A chain of melody that holds her soul—
A song, a tear, and exile ships a-sailing—
    A wan face, patient-eyed, seeking the
      promised goal.

THE BOY'S MOTHER SPEAKS.

IF the Three Blisters of Disgrace were on
      his face,
  And his face is like the sun,
I would efface each trace from its place
  With my kisses, one by one!
If his head were bowed with dread and woe
      and shame,
  And his head is like dull gold,
I'd forget the guilt and shame, and bear his
      share of blame,
  For to love is to forgive when all is told.

TARA OF THE KINGS.

In the great Hall of Tara of the Kings,
Whose fourteen doors stood ever open wide,
With fourteen welcomes to the night and
    day,
The feast was set. White torches flared
    around
From niches in the pillars of red pine,
On Gallant Chiefs and Queenly Women
    there.
The warm light glanced and shone on the
    red gold
Of the rich battle gear of Erinn's Men,
And on the gleaming mail, and wolf skin
    cloaks
Of the sea-roving Giants of the Loch-
    lanachs,
Strong-limbed and fierce were they, with
    eyes that held

The cold, blue sheen of star-lit northern
    deeps,
And teeth that gleamed through flowing,
    tawny beards.
The tables groaned beneath the mighty
    weight
Of ponderous vats of rare and precious
    wines,
And carcases of oxen roasted whole,
Methers of foaming mead went gaily round
From lip to lip, and friend and foe alike
Ate, drank, and quaffed their brimming,
    golden cups,
Forgetting for the moment every wrong
That ever held them sundered. Such the
    law—
No man might draw his sword in. Tara's
    Hall,
In anger on another man, and live.
Then, when the feast was ended, and the
    Bards

And Ollavs skilled in Erinn's ancient lore
Stood in a white-robed throng around the
    Throne
Then was it that a silence deep as death
Fell on that mighty crowd. Outside the
    wind
Stirred in the quicken trees, and to and fro
As if by fairy hands, the banners waved,
And from the farther end of the great Hall
A silver rivulet of music flowed
Into the gloom and silence of the place.
Faintly at first and sweetly, like the song
Of sunbright waters, rang the Harp's clear
    sound;
Louder and louder yet the music swelled,
As Bard and Bard, and Bard took up the
    strain,
And all the burthen of their thrilling song
Was—Tara and the glory of its Kings.
Of Fiann and his Matchless Men they sang,
Of the red rout of battle, and great deeds
Of skill and daring on the tented field.

And then the music took a softer sound—
'Twas Deirdre's sad tale the Minstrels told,
And the dread fate of Usnach's hapless
    sons,
A dirge of sorrow, wailful and desolate—
The saddest tale the world had ever
    heard,—
The women listened with bright, dew-wet
    eyes,
And stern-brow'd warriors stood grim and
    mute
Instinctively each hand went to its spear,
And a low, sorrowful murmur like a caoine
Thrilled through that mighty crowd,
Still the Harps sobbed, and still the Bards
    sang on,
Until with one, grand, maddening crash
    they tore
A mighty chord from out the quivering
    strings,
And the sad tale was told.   Adown the
    Hall

The murmur grew to a tumultuous sound;
The music's fire had quickened hearts and
    brains,
Shield clanged in meeting shield, and
    through the gloom
The torches, in a myriad points of light,
Flashed on bright skians and forests of
    grey spears,
Until the swelling chorus thundered forth,
In one, great, sonorous, deep-throated roar
Of wild applause, its mighty meed of praise
That echoed through the dome of the great
    Hall,
And floated through its fourteen open
    doors.
Out and away into the silent night,
Startling the Red Deer from his ferny lair,
In the green woods round Tara of the
    Kings.

THE WHITE ROAD TO IRELAND.

OCH, the weary's on you, London,
  With your hot streets all ablaze,
In a rain o' yellow sunshine,
  And the drought o' summer days,
Sure I mind me well a white road
  That goes westward to the sea,
And the white road to Ireland
  Is the right road for me.

I'm not mindin' o' the money,
  Here it falls, they say, like rain,
But who'd be thinkin' o' the likes
  That longed for home again?
So tie up your kerchief, Maurya,
  And we'll foot it to the sea,
For the white road to Ireland
  Is the right road for me.

30

There's a brown road in Ireland,
  An' my grief, 'tis steep an' bare,
But through the misty sunshine
  'Tis we'll be climbin' there.
Do you hear the curlew callin'
  As he points out to the sea?
Ah, the brown road in Ireland
  Is the road for you and me.

LAMENT OF A FISHERGIRL FOR HER DROWNED LOVER.

THERE'S a grey cloud hanging o'er Rath
    Cruachan,
Where the grey rocks are grinning through
    the heather,
And there is no sunlight on the hill-roads
Where we two climbed yesterday together.

The hill-winds are moaning like the ocean,
The flame of the gorse has burned low
    down,
But there are three tall white candles
    burning
Where you lie dead and cold in Galway
    town.

There's a dark cloud o'er Connacht of the
    grey stones,
Through a wet mist the boats put out to sea,
And there is no dancing now nor laughter,
There's a grey stone where my heart used
    to be.

The lark is silent now above the heather,
There is silence on the mouth my mouth has
    kissed,
And the yellow light falls where you are
    lying,
But the grey cloud is round me like a mist.

THE WANDERER.

SLANTING rain and white mist falling
   Over the lonely moorland track,
Through purple shadows a grey bird
      calling—
   Ever calling the Wanderer back.

Slanting rain and west wind sighing,
   Out of the hills with an eerie throb,
Lone, grey raths and a Banshee crying,
   Caoining softly with many a sob.

Slanting rain and a wide grey ocean,
   Where the gaunt ship waits like a
      spectral bier,
Shadowy waters in ceaseless motion,
   And grief for a Heart-friend through
      many a year.

MY SHARE O' THE WORLD.

My Share o' the World,
With your brown-head curled—
  Close to my fond heart so cosily,
To the island of dreams,
'Neath the pale moonbeams,
  You've flown on the wings of the Sluah
    Shee.

On the yellow strand
Of that bright dreamland,
  Where day dies never, you'll wander free
Till your boat of pearl—
Like a silver curl
  On the green-streamed sea, bears you
    back to me.

35

Then safe on my bosom,
Oh, pink-white blossom!
  You'll rest till the night's dark win
    furled,
When the dawn of your sleeping—
A blue eye peeping,
  Shall greet me, a leanniv, My S
    the World.

THE DROWNED FISHERMAN.

Because of your love O, Padraic A-Hartigan!
'Tis like some God-forgotten star I am this
  many a day,
Though the life is left within my breast,
  'tis my heart that is far away,
For your bed is the ocean's bed—a wraith
  on a sullen sea,—
And the white bird's call in the darkness
  brings your cry, your cry to me.

My sorrow and my sorrow, O, Padraic A-Hartigan!
My seven curses upon the ocean, and my
  curse on its many ills,
For 'tis I that loved the mountains, God's
  own grey, kindly hills,

But the sea kept a-calling, a-calling you,
    —'twas the woe o' the Banshee's cry,
And I see in my dreams the storm-tossed
    boat and a wan face drifting by.

Youth o' my heart, O, Padraic A-Hartigan!
The day is dreary, the night is long when
    the bay with mist is hid,
And the clank o' oars in the gloaming
    sounds like clay on a coffin lid;
By the swell o' ground seas 'cross the bar,
    through the years shall your caoine
    be cried,
And never till storm and waves are stilled
    shall the tears in my eyes be dried.
Youth, o' my sorrow, O, Padraic A-
Hartigan!

WHITE ROSE OF THE WORLD.

If thou wert mine,

I'd weave three robes of cloud and
glistening dew

Warp of white mist and woof of sunset
hue,

With apple blossoms, faintly red, and
musk,

I'd strew the ways that lead into the dusk

Of deep, cool woods, where dewy fern
frond curls,

Would scatter 'neath thy feet a shower
of pearls,

And steel the moonlight's sheen from the
dim lake,

To pave a silver path for thy dear sake.

If thou wert mine,
 I'd captive make the voice of every bird,
 And wed to each the sweetest, fondest
  word—
 Thy name,—that when they sang their
  song should be,
 Linked with a chain of melodies to thee,
 I'd pluck from out the day its brightest
  hours,
 Wreath them—a diadem of fairest
  flowers,
 When night should come with sable wings
  unfurled—
 To crown thy brow, O, White Rose of the
  World.

If thou wert mine,
 I'd seize the wind (O, throbbing wind of
  sorrow,
 Vex not her soul with whisperings of the
  morrow)
 I'd garner up the radiance of the morn,

The wonder-music of the rustling corn,
To fashion fairyland—the world apart—
And when 'twould fade, I'd house thee in
    my heart.
No impious hand this shrine of thine
    could shatter
O, face divine, O, voice as singing water—
    If thou wert mine.

TO EIRE OF THE SORROWS.

Dearest, when all is done and all is said,
When from Thy head the Crown of Thorns
       is flung,
I shall be happier looking on that Crown
To think that not one word of all I sung
Or said, had helped to press it down
Or bowed in deeper woe Thy Dear Dark
       Head.

A DONEGAL HUSH SONG.

GOD bring you safe from the death sleep
    of night,
        A Leanniv Machree,
        My Heart's Delight,
From the green-hill'd homes of the Sluah
    Shee,
O'er the purple rim of a star-lit sea.
Through a leafy lane, o'er Moy Mell's plain,
Where dew-drops strung on a gossamer
    chain,
From blossomy boughs, swing to and fro,
And a round, red moon hangs low, so low—
God bring you safe through the Night to me.
        My Heart's Delight,
        A Leanniv Machree.

God bring you safe from the death sleep of
    night,
        A Leanniv Machree,
        My Heart's Delight.
From the grey world's edge where the rose-
    dawn sleeps,
Through the white, dream gates where the
    shy day peeps.
Down the silver track of the Morning Star,
To the yellow strand where the white cliffs
    are,
Where each fairy foot in a fairy brogue
Is hastening away to Tir-na-noge,
God bring you safe to the Dawn and me
        My Heart's Delight,
        A Leanniv Machree.

O, FRIEND OF MY HEART.

O, FRIEND of my Heart :
    Like the swish of the wind in the rustling
        grass, like the rhythm of a star,
    Like a singing stream to a thirsty soul in
        a desert place lonely and far.
    Like the deep-throated music of thrushes
        in the windless quiet of days
    Is the breath of your praise.

O, Friend of my Heart !
    'Tis a debt I pay in this telling for hours
        of delight,
    To lay my wreath of bays at your feet I
        would climb afar to your height,
    I would talk the flints with a terrible joy,
        if at the journey's end,
    I would greet you, O Friend !

WHEN I SHALL COME TO YOU.

I SHALL come to you, dear,
In the green o' the year,
With the breeze on the lake,
With the bird in the brake,
When the hedges are gay
With the white o' the May;
I shall come to you bringing
The glad summer's singing
With the lark's silver trills,
With the light on the hills,
And the blue in the valleys,
When through shadowy alleys
Of shimmering larches
And sweet woodbine arches,
We shall walk as of yore
O'er the emerald floor

Of the dim woods, inlaid
With the jasper and jade
Of the green light that falls
Through the aisles, o'er the walls
Of the dark leafy fane,
Weaving shadow and light
Weaving day into night
With warp of gold glances
And woof of green lances,
With the pearl of pale moons
To the rune of old tunes.
With bronze of dark stems,
With the fringe-bordered hems
Of the pine groves that trail
Their green robes down the vale
Through briar, brake and fen
I shall come, dear, again,
When the hedges are gay
With the white o' the May,
I shall come to you bringing
The glad summer's singing,

With the gold iris bending
'Tween the stream's song ascending;
To the song of the breeze
In the low-drooping trees
When the wood-doves are gay
And our hearts glad as they,
In the green o' the year
I shall come to you, dear.

IN IRELAND.

(TO D. R. T.)

WHAT is it you miss, O friend of my heart,
    there by that arid strand,
Where Nilus drags its sun-swept way,
    'tween level banks of sand?
Is it the shadow of clouds of mist that
    shimmer and shine as they pass,
Is it the swish of the slanting rain in the
    long lush wayside grass—
        In Ireland?

Do you miss 'mid the brazen sunshine, and
    the glorious afterglow,
The deep blue of our valleys, the light that
    our dear hills know?
Do you miss 'mid the clamour and bustle
    of the city's echoing ways,
The hush of a loch where the dragon flies
    dart through the soft summer haze—
        In Ireland?

49

Do you miss the long, low wash of the waves
    and the silence that follows after,
Do you miss the startled sea-bird's note, the
    blackbird's chatter and laughter,
And, oh, do you miss the kindly hearts of
    the friends that you love so dear,
Who with straining eyes and eager arms
    are waiting to welcome you here—
    In Ireland?

THE OTHER LIFE.

"The little stone of truth rolling through the many ages of the world has gathered and grown grey with the thick mosses of romance and superstition. But tradition must always have the little stone of truth for its kernel, and perhaps he who rejects all is likelier to be wrong than even foolish folk like myself, who love to believe all, and who tread the new paths, thinking ever of the ancient stories."

'Tis but a vain, unreal thing, and yet, and
    yet
Is it that I remember dimly, or but half
    forget
That other Life that comes in dreams to
    me
Over the Hills of Silence from an unknown
    sea?
It seems of old I've wandered through a
    land

Whose gates of pearl ope on a golden
    strand,
And the far spreading boughs of blossomed
    trees
Cover the sward with shimmering traceries;
Where feathery grasses fringe dark pools
    —a dream—
Across whose placid bosoms white wings
    gleam,
And days drift by as dreams across the
    night—
Swift days that end in long nights of
    delight.
In days long dead I've roamed, and by my
    side
Was Emer of the Faithful Heart—
    Cuchulain's bride,
No longer mourning for her valiant Hound,
For close about his neck her arms were
    wound,
And Meave of Cruachan, dark-browed,
    mighty queen,
Her crimson mantle trailing o'er the green,

Passed onward with a gracious, shadowy
    smile,
And a Brown Bull lowed deep in a wood-
    land aisle,
Beneath the quicken trees where Grainne
    laid,
Her lips to Diarmuid's, and with that kiss
    betrayed
Her lover and her lord; I walked with
    Niav,
Ere yet she drew sad Oissin o'er the wave—
Niav of the golden head and witching
    words,
Whose voice had caught the tones of
    Angus' birds.
In that old life when love itself was life,
I've lived and loved and gloried in its
    strife.
Perchance I do but dream, and at the ford,
Never fell Ferdiad by his heart-friend's
    sword:

Perchance I do but dream, and De
  never
Of all sad songs sang yet the saddest
Perchance I do but dream—and yet,
  yet,
Is it that I remember dimly, or but
  forget?

SPRING.

A SLENDER blade of grass beside a stone,
A gleam of sunshine 'tween the narrow
    roofs,
A solitary seed of grass wind sown
Beneath the trampling of impatient hoofs.
The happy children in the windy street
Play Ring o' Roses, gambol, laugh and
    sing.
Across the blue a flash of wings—tweet!
    tweet!
And so 'tis Spring.

A DREAM.

It was fanned of unseen fires,
　　The fires that chasten and smart.
Of my seared soul's white flame,
　　And the red flame of my heart.

Of the fierce white heat of Youth,
　　And the glow of its passion fire
Youth, the Dreamer, who fashions
　　And colours the Heart's Desire.

With dead dreams half forgot
　　The living ore was wrought
Till it shaped itself in my heart,
　　Took form and came forth—a Thought.

It burned as a star in the dark
　　In its travail hour of birth,
As a diamond deep in the womb
　　Of the fruitful red-brown earth.

Like a rhythm of joyous sound,
　Like a gleam of tremulous light,
It fell on men's wond'ring ears,
　It glowed and sang in their sight.

They pondered it o'er and o'er,
　They sundered it part from part,
The song that was half my soul,
　The word that was all my heart.

"He has lost the Clue," they said—
　"The Clue and the Golden Key."
But it—it was all my life
　For it came from the Soul o' Me.

THE JOY OF GIVING.

GIVE of the gold whereof your heart is
    made
  To those poor bankrupt ones who have
    no store
Of love or joy or hope, whose sorry trade
  Is digging in the dust-heaps for the
    phantom ore.

Give your tears' balm to every lonely soul
  Who yearns for a dead day, a little while
When Death shall add a name to the long
    roll
  You can then answer with a tearless
    smile.

Give loving faith and truth and sympathy
  To those who in the furnace have been
    tried,
And you shall walk in beauty and shall see
  Life, Love and Death by gladness
    glorified.

58

THE SONG O' TH' SAY.

Night an' morn it's on me, this wearyin'
    for th' say
An' th' swish o' breakers an' th' clank o'
    oars in Inver Bay;
'Tis a sin to be grievin', they tell me, but,
    sure, 'twas God above,
That put in my heart th' song that fills it
    with longin' an' love.

Many's th' year since I left it, th' home so
    purty, so poor,
An' took th' windin' casaun that led to th'
    worl' across th' moor,
But first I went down th' beach to kiss th'
    ledge by th' shore,
Ah, God! I can feel th' salt on my lips th'
    day an' evermore.

A 'kerchief o' spotted red held all my store,
    an' a shell,
An' a song o' th' say within it, th' music I
    loved so well;
Now when th' childre are weary I take
    them up on my breast,
An' th' song that th' shell keeps singin'
    soothes each weeshy head to rest.

'Tis many's th' year, an' I'm thinkin' will
    th' longing ever be stilled,
For I'm here in th' lonely city yet, an' my
    dream is unfulfilled.
But though 'tis years since it sang to me,
    my heart knows that some day,
When life is over, as th' voice of a lover,
    I'll hear th' song o' th' say.

THANKSGIVING.

THANK God for the Trees and the Flowers
   And the Blue, Blue Sky,
Thank God for the Happy Hours
   And Hope that can never die.
Thank God, though the Way be long
   For Joy when the Journey ends,
Thank God for the Gift of Song,
   And, O! Thank God for my Friends.

EMER AT THE GRAVE OF CUCHULAIN.

" *Love of my life,*" she said.
As she went down into the new-made grave,
And laid her mouth close to his cold mouth,
And never did sweeter blossoms swing
    together
In the honey-sweet and breath-warm
    breezes of the south.

" *My friend, my sweetheart,*" she said,
And the beauty of her warmed the cold,
    dead clay,
And her voice's music filled Death's lonely
    house,
And her, white arms, like swans through
    sunny waters
Tossed her hair's golden spray above his
    breast, and o'er his death-dark
    brows.

" *My one choice of Erinn's men* " she said,
As she laid her length along that narrow
    place,
With bitter crying and with many a moan,
And, 'twas what she said, twining his dead
    arms around her,
" *Since you are gone from me, there is no*
    word better with me than, ochon!"

SPRING IN THE CITY.

"THERE'S a breath of Spring in the air
    to-day"
Called out my neighbour across the way,
And the words with their gladdening
    message wound
Through the city's hollow with joyous
    sound.
       Down the echoing street
       Came flying feet,
And daffodils leaned from a window sill,
Where the merry children laughed loud
    and shrill,
       Youth and Joy,
       A girl and a boy,
       With a hoop and a ball
       And a whoop and a call

To the sunbeams and breeze, all friends
    together
Went dancing into the wine-like ether,
And my heart, atune, sang adown the way
To the Yellowbill's note on the topmost
    spray,
And my soul seemed aglow at the greeting
    gay,
" There's a breath of Spring in the air
    to-day."

EIRE'S AWAKENING.

Saw you the Wraith-light flicker and fail,
  Men of the Glens, through the blinding
    sleet?
Saw you a cloud o'er the grey sky sail,
  And wrap the day in its winding sheet?
Heard you the roar of the tempest's breath,
  Lashing the waves in its passionate
    scorning?
Felt you the stillness as deep as Death?
'Twas but the Hour of our Eire's mourning.

Heard you the woe of the Caoiner's tale,
  Men of the Glens, in your eerie shieling?
Heard you the sound of the Banshee's wail,
  You of the Hills, o'er the upland steal-
    ing?

Saw you the wan light grey and cold
   Break in the East, at the Day Star's
      peeping?
Saw you his glory of crimson and gold?
   'Twas but the Hour of our Eire's sleep-
      ing.

Heard you a song by a Siren sung,
   Men of the Glens, through the woodland
      ringing,
In the liquid tones of the Gaelic tongue,
   Sweet as the sunlit streamlet's singing?
See you a myriad, stern-brow'd men,
   The very earth 'neath their grand tread
      shaking?
Seeking the Singer through brake and fen,
   This, this is the Hour of our Eire's
      waking.

THE QUICKENBERRIES OF DOOROS.

THE Quickenberries of Dooros
  Hang heavy-clustered, dull red as drops
    of blood,
    Crimson amongst green branches,
    scarlet against the sky,
  And who shall taste of their magic shall
    know all evil and good
    Him shall no power destroy, nor
    sorrow nor scaith come nigh.

I walk through low, grey meadows, and
    ever a kind one stoops
    To lead me to higher pastures, sun-
    lighted, shadow-forgot,
Where the pines trail feathery robes and
    the heavy fruitage droops,
    Where the olden silence is flowing and
    the waves of time beat not.

I have known the laughter of Love and
    have seen the folly of Hate
    Clear as the stars that travel the dome
    of God's floor o'erhead,
I laugh at the little ways of Men, the
    pigmy antics of Fate,
    For I dream old dreams of delight and
    live in days that are dead.

The Quickenberries of Dooros
    Hang heavy-clustered, dull red as drops
    of blood,
    Crimson amongst green lances, scarlet
    'mid bronze and gold,
And who shall taste of their magic shall
    know all evil and good;
    Him shall no fret disturb, he shall
    laugh when the world is old.

THE PRIMAL SILENCE.

(A FRAGMENT.)

WHEN Satan laughed behind the apple-tree
In Eden was heard no more of Melody,
A midnight silence fell across the noon,
From grove and glade rang out no sweet
      bird-tune,
Deep in the flowering grasses brute by
      brute,
Lay still as death, the singing streams were
      mute,
And where the reeds and brook-fed rushes
      swayed,
The minstral breeze no wonder-music made,
The soaring lark, poising on tremulous
      wing,
Dropped from the sky, a songless, silent
      thing,

And where a melody of waters played,
Silence a finger on their glad lips laid,
And when thro' the great hush that
    laughter jarred
Man blushed for shame of that hour evil
    starred,
And hid himself in silence, sore afraid,
Dreading to hear the Voice of Him who
    made
The glad days of the World, and every leaf
That covered him to hide his fear and
    grief,
And every beast and bird and blade of
    grass
Each living thing that in the Garden was
Each tree and flower and stem and seeding
    pod
Listened to hear the awful Voice of God,
Then where an Angel stood with fiery
    sword
Bearing aloft the Mandate of the Lord.

Two crouching figures passed, and the
      sun
Sank on that Day of Doom into oblivi
And God hung out a branch of silent st
Beyond that Portal's menace of Red B
Where, to the awful vastness of dim, si]
      spaces,
The   Wanderers   turned   their   sorr
      stricken faces.

DAFFODILS.

CAVALIERS out of the Age of Gold
Why come ye trooping, a myriad fold?
Gaily riding adown the years
With golden helmets and grey-green
    spears.

Wherefore, O Gallants, brave and bold,
Ride ye out of the Age of Gold
Into a world so cold and grey?
Way, for the Golden Men, make way!

Speed ye forth at some King's behest,
Or some high, noble and knightly quest?
To succour and save in this forest shady
Some high-born captive lady.

We come at the call of our Ladye, Spring.
Largess of gold for grace we bring,
To her Court we ride over mead and wold,
Heralding in the Age of Gold.

ASTHOREEN.

OH, the hills are fair in Erin, green and
gold each towering crest,
And the laughing streamlet flashes
through the heather in its glee.
And the nursling of the waters on its ocean
mother's breast
Is cradled to the music of the sunbright
sea;
And I look across the valley where the
reaper 'mid the grain
To the swinging of his sickle sings a
careless, happy tune.
And I wonder if in Erin we shall ever meet
again
When the throstle's note is heard among
the glancing green of June.
Asthoreen! Asthoreen!

74

Heed you not my sad heart's pleading?
    It goes out across the green sea that for-
        ever lies between,
And the burthen of its message that the
    breezes bear unheeding :
    Shall we meet again in Erin when the
    hills are fair and green?

Oh, the hills are green in Erin, and the
    fragrant breezes blow
    Through the tangled briar and bracken
    where the fairies vigil keep :
Gleam the ruddy quickenberries 'gainst the
    azure sky aglow
    Sweet as blushes red and radiant on the
    cheek of child asleep.
And my heart is filled with gladness, and
    the earth with joy is teeming,
    And my eager eyes look out beyond the
    green sea's crystal sheen;
For the sigh of breeze and song of bird and
    sunlight softly streaming

All say we'll meet in Erin when the
    are fair and green.
        Asthoreen! Asthoreen!
Heed you not my glad heart's swellin
    It goes out across the green sea that
        ever lies between,
And the burthen of its message to
        breezes I am telling :
    We shall meet again in Erin when
        hills are fair and green.

THE WOE OF ALL THE WORLD.

THERE is no beauty in the world—Deirdre
    being dead—
And Ferdiad's white limbs hid in the red-
    dening stream.
The birds of Angus only know Moy Mell,
And earth's old ways are desolate, now men
    save
And hoard the joy and laughter of their
    lives
To lavish tears alone on what they love.
Oh, I have sat with friends throughout fair
    hours
And laughed and sang and watched their
    faces glow
Like happy children round a ruddy fire.

77

And I have seen those faces pale and set
When a sad viol through the silence sobbed,
And looked, to see men's souls laid stark
        and bare
In their own sight, to their great wonder-
        ment
When the sweet music trembled and died
        out,
And I have seen the crimson wave of dawn
Cast up the beautiful, white corse of day
Before a careless crowd, and while the
        laugh
And song alternate flowed from wine wet
        lips,
Have seen the tears for youth's lost
        fragrant grace
Slow coursing down the fair cheek of a
        friend.

NOTES

How Diarmuid got his Love-Spot.

Diarmuid ever after wore a cap to conceal his love-spot, but, once in endeavouring to separate the hounds that were quarrelling over the remnants of a feast at Tara, his cap fell off, whereupon Grainne saw the mark and gave him her love. She persuaded him to fly with her from Tara, and it was while defending her from a wild boar on the mountain of Ben Bulhan that he received his death wound.

Grainne. After the Death of Diarmuid.

Grainne, the daughter of King Cormac, was betrothed to Fionn Mac Cumhal, but falling in love with Diarmuid O'Duibhne, a Captain of the Fianna, persuaded him to elope with her. The "Pursuit of Diarmuid and Grainne" by the vengeful Fionn forms the subject of one of the Bardic tales of Erin. Diarmuid was killed by a wild boar in the Woods of Ben Bulban.

When Seumas Mac-an-Ree played "The Coulin."

Jimmy Mac Ilroy, a traditional fiddler of Cushendall, Co. Antrim.

The Boy's Mother Speaks.

When Meave sent out the Druids and the Satirists to bring Ferdiad to fight against his friend and companion, Cuchulain, she told them

if he would not come to raise the three blisters of
disgrace on his face, Shame and Blemish and
Reproach, so that if he did not die on the moment,
he would be dead at the end of nine days.

My Share o' the World.
The Sluah Shee is the Fairy Host.

A Donegal Hush Song.
Moy Mell is the Honey-sweet Plain of Fairy-
land.

Emer at the Grave of Cuchulain.
Emer was the beautiful and devoted wife of
Cuchulain, the Hound of Ulster.

The Quickenberries of Dooros.
It was to the Forest of Dooros Diarmuid and
Grainne fled for refuge when pursued by Fionn,
following their flight from Tara.   Thither, too,
the incensed Leader of the Fianna and his followers
penetrated, and nearly every incident, tragic or
romantic which ensued, is associated with the
quickenberries, or berries of the rowan-tree, which
in Druidic times bore a mystic significance.

The Woe of all the World.
The kisses of Angus, the Irish god of Youth and
Love, turned to white birds which circled about his
head. Angus Og, son of the Dagda, was the Irish
Hermes, and master of many arts.

CPSIA information can be obtained
at www.ICGtesting.com
Printed in the USA
LVOW05s0841110617
537711LV00028B/516/P